Password Keeper

By

Mystic Art Glitters

Dates to remember

January

February

March

April

May

June

Dates to remember

July

August

September

October

November

December

NAME:

WEBSITE:

USERNAME:

PASSWORD:

NOTES:

NAME:

WEBSITE:

USERNAME:

PASSWORD:

NOTES:

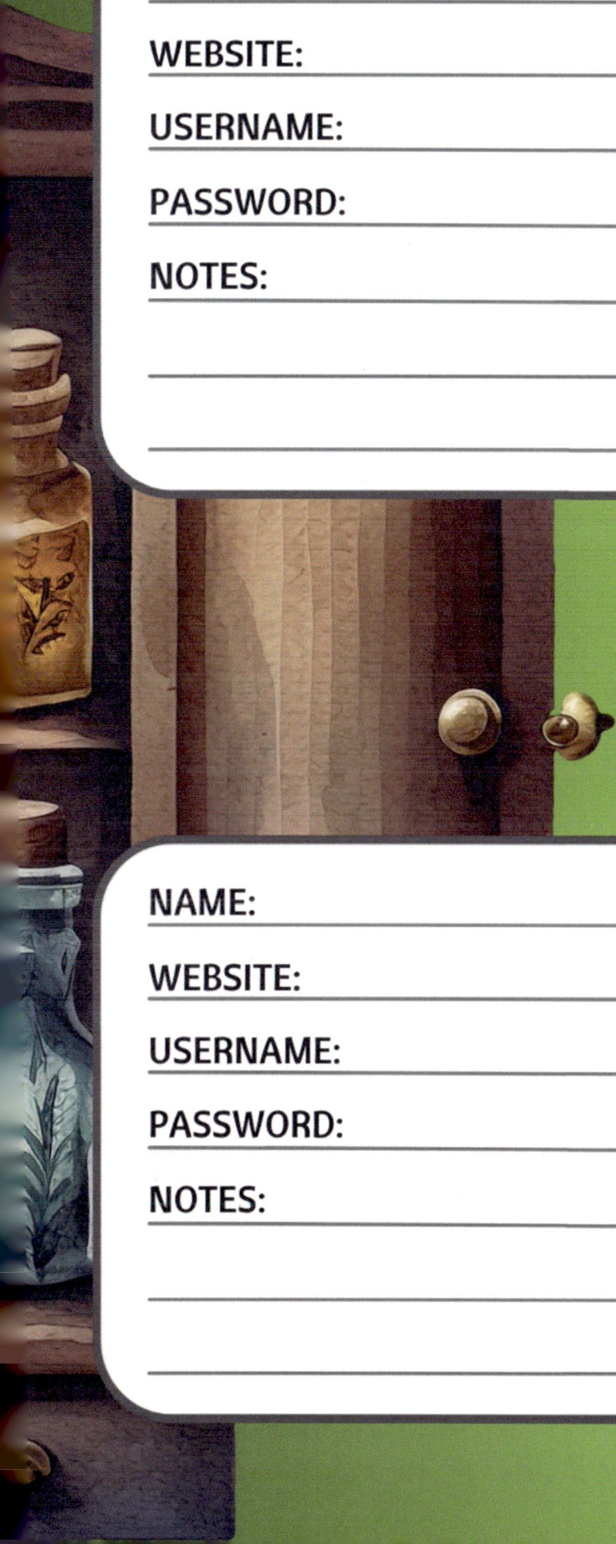

NAME:

WEBSITE:

USERNAME:

PASSWORD:

NOTES:

NAME:

WEBSITE:

USERNAME:

PASSWORD:

NOTES:

NAME:

WEBSITE:

USERNAME:

PASSWORD:

NOTES:

NAME:

WEBSITE:

USERNAME:

PASSWORD:

NOTES:

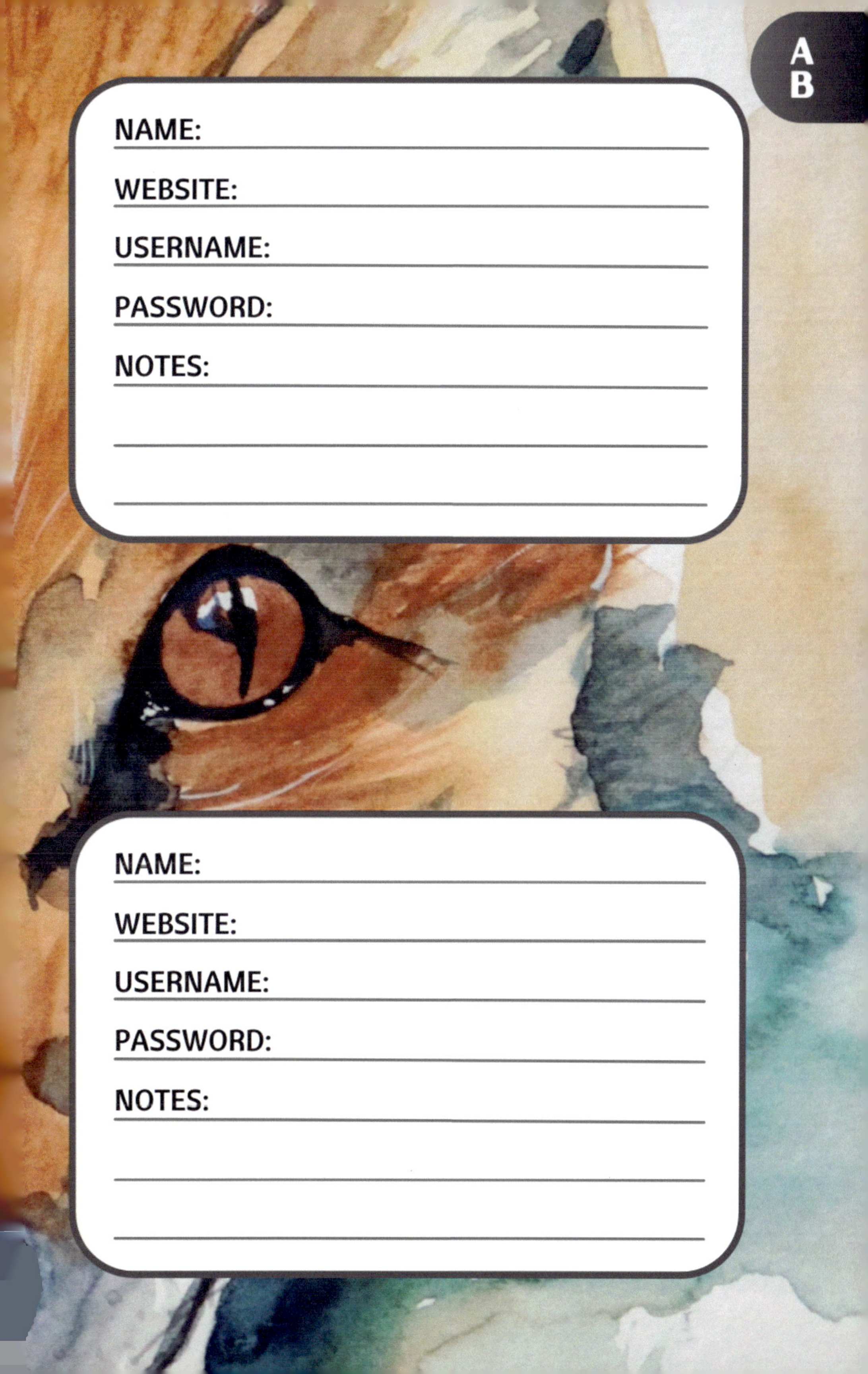

NAME: ____________________

WEBSITE: ____________________

USERNAME: ____________________

PASSWORD: ____________________

NOTES: ____________________

____

____

NAME: ____________________

WEBSITE: ____________________

USERNAME: ____________________

PASSWORD: ____________________

NOTES: ____________________

____

____

NAME:

WEBSITE:

USERNAME:

PASSWORD:

NOTES:

NAME:

WEBSITE:

USERNAME:

PASSWORD:

NOTES:

NAME:

WEBSITE:

USERNAME:

PASSWORD:

NOTES:

NAME:

WEBSITE:

USERNAME:

PASSWORD:

NOTES:

NAME: ______________________

WEBSITE: ______________________

USERNAME: ______________________

PASSWORD: ______________________

NOTES: ______________________

____

____

NAME: ______________________

WEBSITE: ______________________

USERNAME: ______________________

PASSWORD: ______________________

NOTES: ______________________

____

____

NAME:

WEBSITE:

USERNAME:

PASSWORD:

NOTES:

NAME:

WEBSITE:

USERNAME:

PASSWORD:

NOTES:

NAME: ______________________

WEBSITE: ______________________

USERNAME: ______________________

PASSWORD: ______________________

NOTES: ______________________

____

____

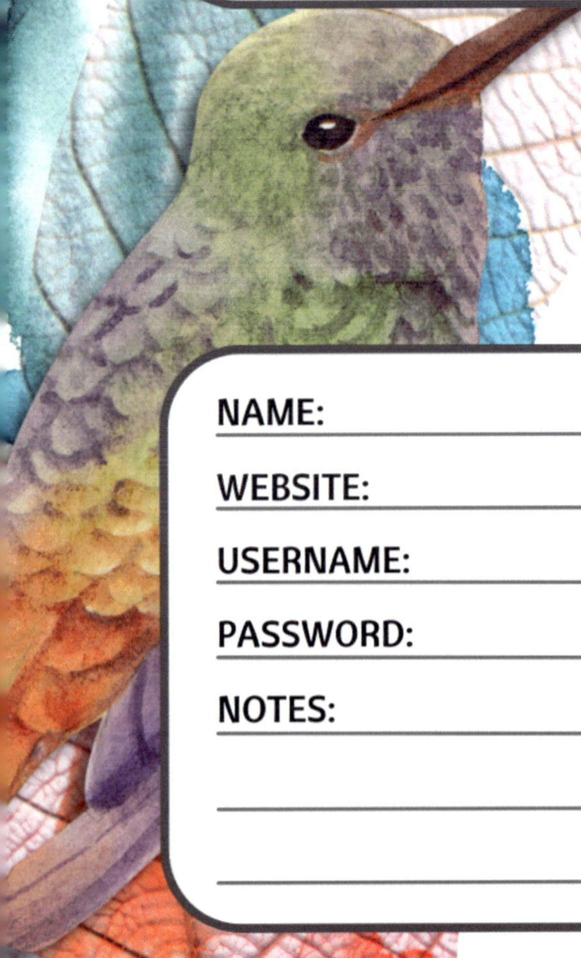

NAME: ______________________

WEBSITE: ______________________

USERNAME: ______________________

PASSWORD: ______________________

NOTES: ______________________

____

____

NAME:

WEBSITE:

USERNAME:

PASSWORD:

NOTES:

NAME:

WEBSITE:

USERNAME:

PASSWORD:

NOTES:

NAME:

WEBSITE:

USERNAME:

PASSWORD:

NOTES:

NAME:

WEBSITE:

USERNAME:

PASSWORD:

NOTES:

NAME:

WEBSITE:

USERNAME:

PASSWORD:

NOTES:

NAME:

WEBSITE:

USERNAME:

PASSWORD:

NOTES:

NAME:

WEBSITE:

USERNAME:

PASSWORD:

NOTES:

NAME:

WEBSITE:

USERNAME:

PASSWORD:

NOTES:

NAME:

WEBSITE:

USERNAME:

PASSWORD:

NOTES:

NAME:

WEBSITE:

USERNAME:

PASSWORD:

NOTES:

NAME:

WEBSITE:

USERNAME:

PASSWORD:

NOTES:

NAME:

WEBSITE:

USERNAME:

PASSWORD:

NOTES:

NAME:

WEBSITE:

USERNAME:

PASSWORD:

NOTES:

NAME:

WEBSITE:

USERNAME:

PASSWORD:

NOTES:

NAME:

WEBSITE:

USERNAME:

PASSWORD:

NOTES:

NAME:

WEBSITE:

USERNAME:

PASSWORD:

NOTES:

NAME:

WEBSITE:

USERNAME:

PASSWORD:

NOTES:

NAME:

WEBSITE:

USERNAME:

PASSWORD:

NOTES:

NAME:

WEBSITE:

USERNAME:

PASSWORD:

NOTES:

NAME:

WEBSITE:

USERNAME:

PASSWORD:

NOTES:

NAME:

WEBSITE:

USERNAME:

PASSWORD:

NOTES:

NAME:

WEBSITE:

USERNAME:

PASSWORD:

NOTES:

NAME:

WEBSITE:

USERNAME:

PASSWORD:

NOTES:

NAME:

WEBSITE:

USERNAME:

PASSWORD:

NOTES:

NAME:

WEBSITE:

USERNAME:

PASSWORD:

NOTES:

NAME:

WEBSITE:

USERNAME:

PASSWORD:

NOTES:

NAME:

WEBSITE:

USERNAME:

PASSWORD:

NOTES:

NAME:

WEBSITE:

USERNAME:

PASSWORD:

NOTES:

NAME:

WEBSITE:

USERNAME:

PASSWORD:

NOTES:

E
F

NAME:

WEBSITE:

USERNAME:

PASSWORD:

NOTES:

NAME:

WEBSITE:

USERNAME:

PASSWORD:

NOTES:

NAME:

WEBSITE:

USERNAME:

PASSWORD:

NOTES:

NAME:

WEBSITE:

USERNAME:

PASSWORD:

NOTES:

E
F

NAME:

WEBSITE:

USERNAME:

PASSWORD:

NOTES:

NAME:

WEBSITE:

USERNAME:

PASSWORD:

NOTES:

NAME:

WEBSITE:

USERNAME:

PASSWORD:

NOTES:

NAME:

WEBSITE:

USERNAME:

PASSWORD:

NOTES:

NAME:

WEBSITE:

USERNAME:

PASSWORD:

NOTES:

NAME:

WEBSITE:

USERNAME:

PASSWORD:

NOTES:

NAME:

WEBSITE:

USERNAME:

PASSWORD:

NOTES:

NAME:

WEBSITE:

USERNAME:

PASSWORD:

NOTES:

NAME:

WEBSITE:

USERNAME:

PASSWORD:

NOTES:

NAME: ____________________

WEBSITE: ____________________

USERNAME: ____________________

PASSWORD: ____________________

NOTES: ____________________

NAME: ____________________

WEBSITE: ____________________

USERNAME: ____________________

PASSWORD: ____________________

NOTES: ____________________

NAME: ____________________

WEBSITE: ____________________

USERNAME: ____________________

PASSWORD: ____________________

NOTES: ____________________

____

____

NAME: ____________________

WEBSITE: ____________________

USERNAME: ____________________

PASSWORD: ____________________

NOTES: ____________________

____

____

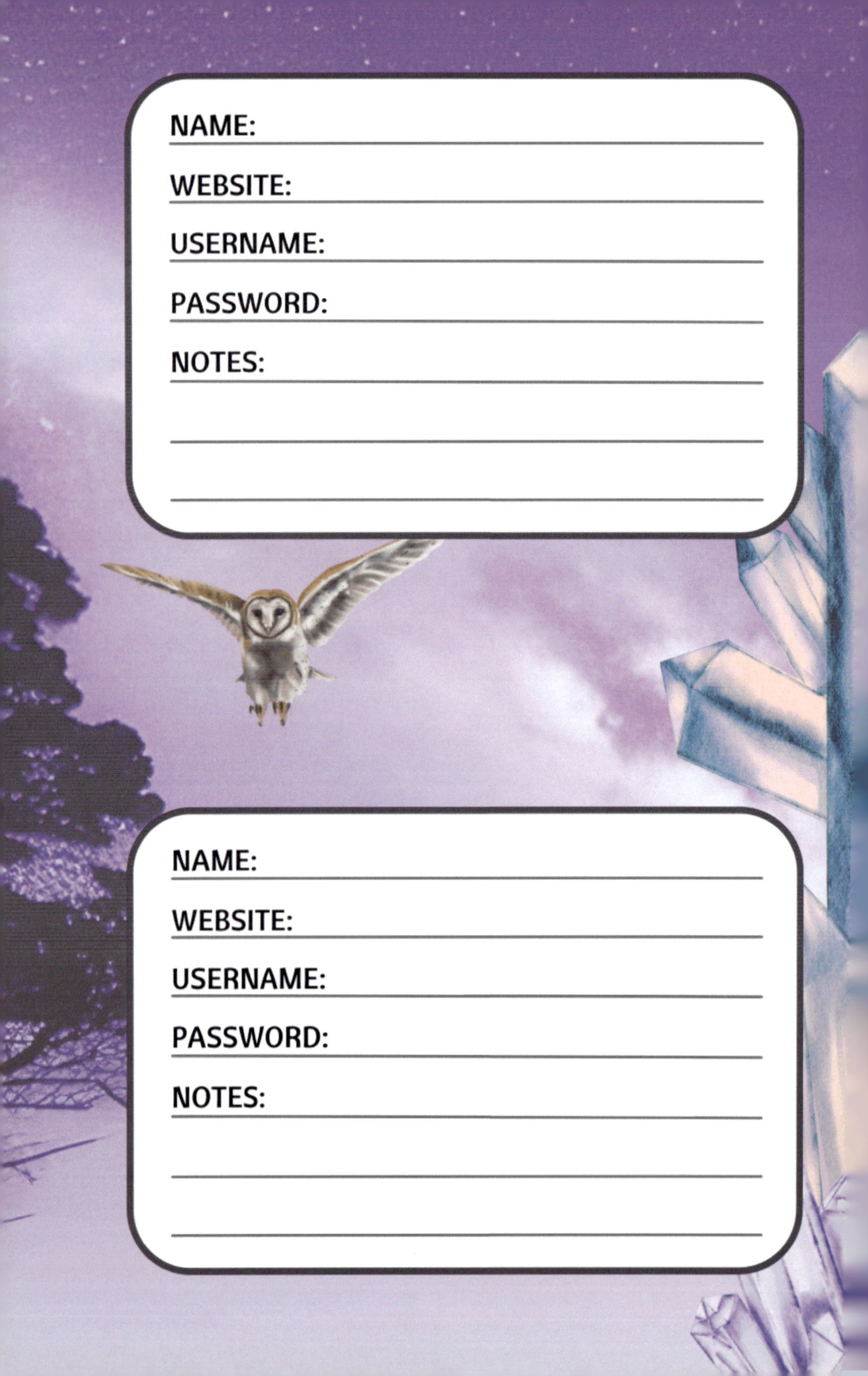

NAME: ______________________

WEBSITE: ______________________

USERNAME: ______________________

PASSWORD: ______________________

NOTES: ______________________

____

____

NAME: ______________________

WEBSITE: ______________________

USERNAME: ______________________

PASSWORD: ______________________

NOTES: ______________________

____

____

NAME:

WEBSITE:

USERNAME:

PASSWORD:

NOTES:

NAME:

WEBSITE:

USERNAME:

PASSWORD:

NOTES:

NAME:

WEBSITE:

USERNAME:

PASSWORD:

NOTES:

NAME:

WEBSITE:

USERNAME:

PASSWORD:

NOTES:

NAME:

WEBSITE:

USERNAME:

PASSWORD:

NOTES:

NAME:

WEBSITE:

USERNAME:

PASSWORD:

NOTES:

NAME:

WEBSITE:

USERNAME:

PASSWORD:

NOTES:

NAME:

WEBSITE:

USERNAME:

PASSWORD:

NOTES:

NAME:

WEBSITE:

USERNAME:

PASSWORD:

NOTES:

NAME:

WEBSITE:

USERNAME:

PASSWORD:

NOTES:

NAME:

WEBSITE:

USERNAME:

PASSWORD:

NOTES:

NAME:

WEBSITE:

USERNAME:

PASSWORD:

NOTES:

NAME:

WEBSITE:

USERNAME:

PASSWORD:

NOTES:

NAME:

WEBSITE:

USERNAME:

PASSWORD:

NOTES:

NAME:

WEBSITE:

USERNAME:

PASSWORD:

NOTES:

NAME:

WEBSITE:

USERNAME:

PASSWORD:

NOTES:

NAME:

WEBSITE:

USERNAME:

PASSWORD:

NOTES:

NAME:

WEBSITE:

USERNAME:

PASSWORD:

NOTES:

NAME:

WEBSITE:

USERNAME:

PASSWORD:

NOTES:

NAME:

WEBSITE:

USERNAME:

PASSWORD:

NOTES:

NAME:

WEBSITE:

USERNAME:

PASSWORD:

NOTES:

J

NAME:

WEBSITE:

USERNAME:

PASSWORD:

NOTES:

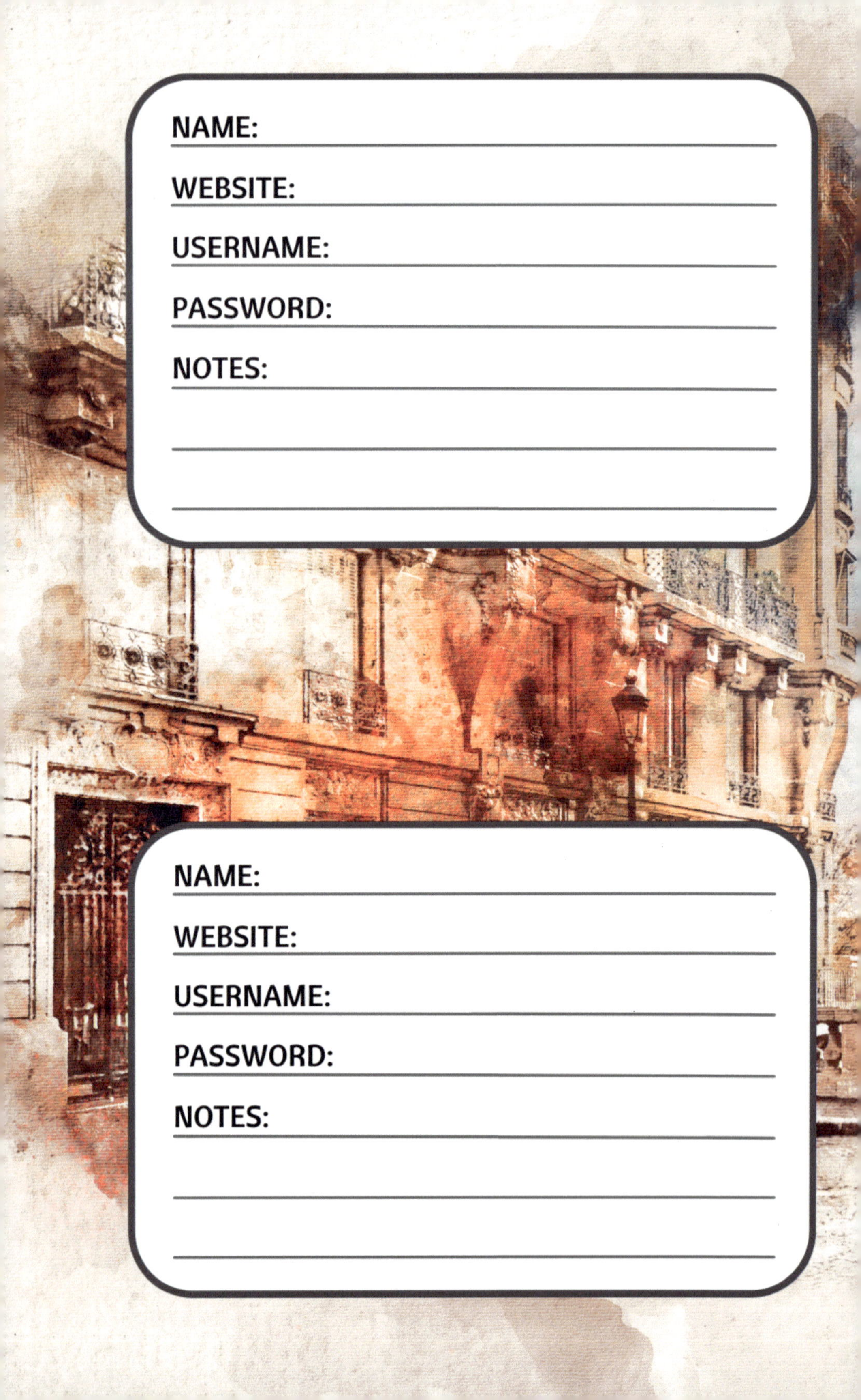

NAME:

WEBSITE:

USERNAME:

PASSWORD:

NOTES:

NAME:

WEBSITE:

USERNAME:

PASSWORD:

NOTES:

J

NAME:

WEBSITE:

USERNAME:

PASSWORD:

NOTES:

NAME:

WEBSITE:

USERNAME:

PASSWORD:

NOTES:

NAME:

WEBSITE:

USERNAME:

PASSWORD:

NOTES:

NAME:

WEBSITE:

USERNAME:

PASSWORD:

NOTES:

NAME:

WEBSITE:

USERNAME:

PASSWORD:

NOTES:

NAME:

WEBSITE:

USERNAME:

PASSWORD:

NOTES:

NAME:

WEBSITE:

USERNAME:

PASSWORD:

NOTES:

NAME:

WEBSITE:

USERNAME:

PASSWORD:

NOTES:

NAME:

WEBSITE:

USERNAME:

PASSWORD:

NOTES:

NAME:

WEBSITE:

USERNAME:

PASSWORD:

NOTES:

NAME:

WEBSITE:

USERNAME:

PASSWORD:

NOTES:

NAME:

WEBSITE:

USERNAME:

PASSWORD:

NOTES:

NAME:

WEBSITE:

USERNAME:

PASSWORD:

NOTES:

K
L

NAME:

WEBSITE:

USERNAME:

PASSWORD:

NOTES:

NAME:

WEBSITE:

USERNAME:

PASSWORD:

NOTES:

NAME:

WEBSITE:

USERNAME:

PASSWORD:

NOTES:

NAME:

WEBSITE:

USERNAME:

PASSWORD:

NOTES:

NAME:

WEBSITE:

USERNAME:

PASSWORD:

NOTES:

NAME:

WEBSITE:

USERNAME:

PASSWORD:

NOTES:

NAME:

WEBSITE:

USERNAME:

PASSWORD:

NOTES:

NAME:

WEBSITE:

USERNAME:

PASSWORD:

NOTES:

K
L

NAME:

WEBSITE:

USERNAME:

PASSWORD:

NOTES:

NAME:

WEBSITE:

USERNAME:

PASSWORD:

NOTES:

NAME:

WEBSITE:

USERNAME:

PASSWORD:

NOTES:

NAME:

WEBSITE:

USERNAME:

PASSWORD:

NOTES:

NAME:

WEBSITE:

USERNAME:

PASSWORD:

NOTES:

NAME:

WEBSITE:

USERNAME:

PASSWORD:

NOTES:

NAME:

WEBSITE:

USERNAME:

PASSWORD:

NOTES:

NAME:

WEBSITE:

USERNAME:

PASSWORD:

NOTES:

NAME:

WEBSITE:

USERNAME:

PASSWORD:

NOTES:

NAME: ______________________

WEBSITE: ______________________

USERNAME: ______________________

PASSWORD: ______________________

NOTES: ______________________

____

____

NAME: ______________________

WEBSITE: ______________________

USERNAME: ______________________

PASSWORD: ______________________

NOTES: ______________________

____

____

NAME:

WEBSITE:

USERNAME:

PASSWORD:

NOTES:

M N

NAME:

WEBSITE:

USERNAME:

PASSWORD:

NOTES:

NAME:

WEBSITE:

USERNAME:

PASSWORD:

NOTES:

NAME:

WEBSITE:

USERNAME:

PASSWORD:

NOTES:

NAME:

WEBSITE:

USERNAME:

PASSWORD:

NOTES:

NAME:

WEBSITE:

USERNAME:

PASSWORD:

NOTES:

NAME:

WEBSITE:

USERNAME:

PASSWORD:

NOTES:

NAME:

WEBSITE:

USERNAME:

PASSWORD:

NOTES:

NAME:

WEBSITE:

USERNAME:

PASSWORD:

NOTES:

NAME:

WEBSITE:

USERNAME:

PASSWORD:

NOTES:

NAME:

WEBSITE:

USERNAME:

PASSWORD:

NOTES:

NAME:

WEBSITE:

USERNAME:

PASSWORD:

NOTES:

NAME:

WEBSITE:

USERNAME:

PASSWORD:

NOTES:

M
N

NAME:

WEBSITE:

USERNAME:

PASSWORD:

NOTES:

NAME:

WEBSITE:

USERNAME:

PASSWORD:

NOTES:

NAME:

WEBSITE:

USERNAME:

PASSWORD:

NOTES:

NAME:

WEBSITE:

USERNAME:

PASSWORD:

NOTES:

M N

NAME:

WEBSITE:

USERNAME:

PASSWORD:

NOTES:

NAME:

WEBSITE:

USERNAME:

PASSWORD:

NOTES:

NAME:

WEBSITE:

USERNAME:

PASSWORD:

NOTES:

NAME:

WEBSITE:

USERNAME:

PASSWORD:

NOTES:

O
P

NAME:

WEBSITE:

USERNAME:

PASSWORD:

NOTES:

NAME:

WEBSITE:

USERNAME:

PASSWORD:

NOTES:

NAME:

WEBSITE:

USERNAME:

PASSWORD:

NOTES:

NAME:

WEBSITE:

USERNAME:

PASSWORD:

NOTES:

NAME:

WEBSITE:

USERNAME:

PASSWORD:

NOTES:

NAME:

WEBSITE:

USERNAME:

PASSWORD:

NOTES:

NAME:

WEBSITE:

USERNAME:

PASSWORD:

NOTES:

NAME:

WEBSITE:

USERNAME:

PASSWORD:

NOTES:

NAME:

WEBSITE:

USERNAME:

PASSWORD:

NOTES:

NAME:

WEBSITE:

USERNAME:

PASSWORD:

NOTES:

NAME:

WEBSITE:

USERNAME:

PASSWORD:

NOTES:

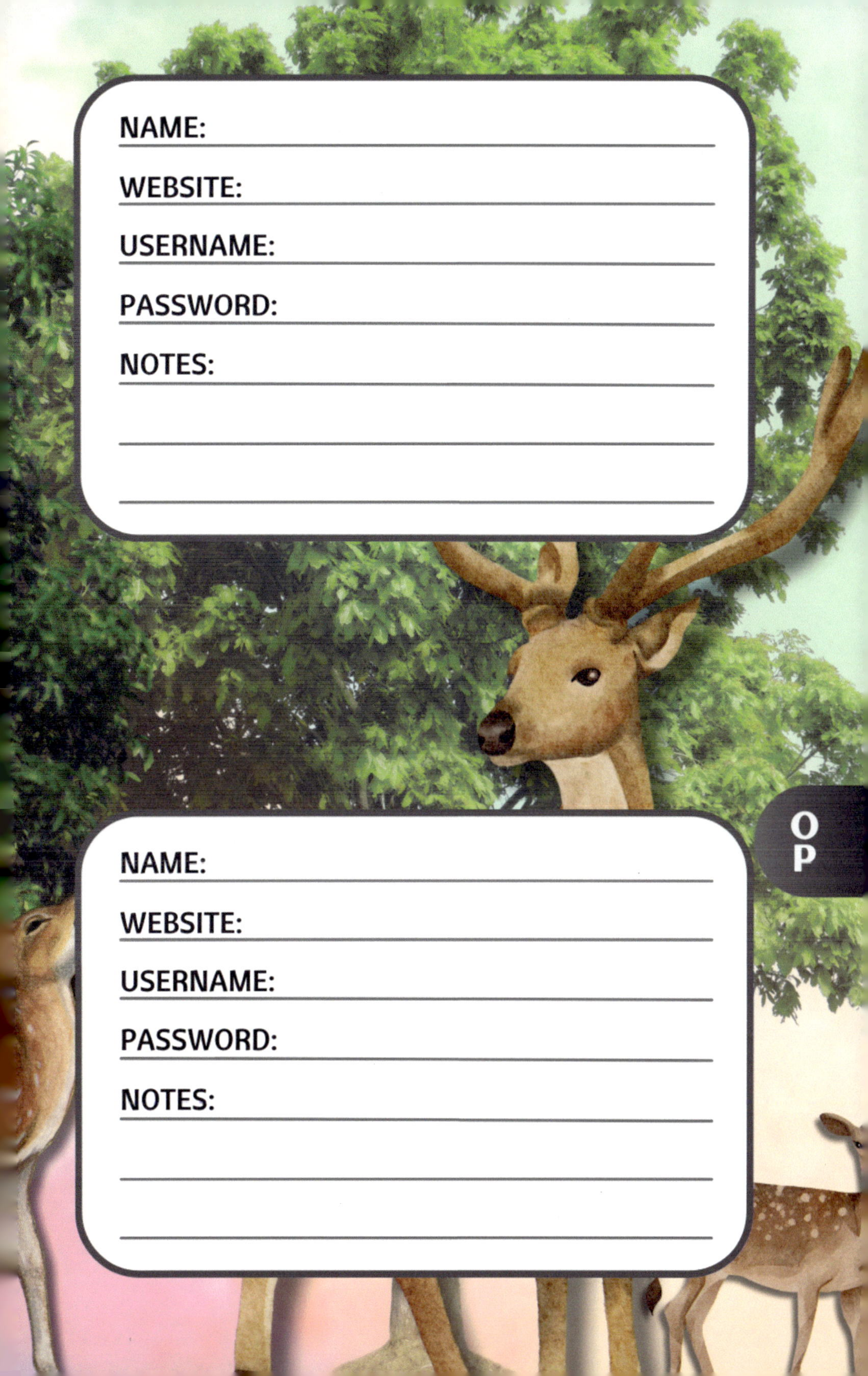

NAME:

WEBSITE:

USERNAME:

PASSWORD:

NOTES:

NAME:

WEBSITE:

USERNAME:

PASSWORD:

NOTES:

NAME:

WEBSITE:

USERNAME:

PASSWORD:

NOTES:

NAME:

WEBSITE:

USERNAME:

PASSWORD:

NOTES:

NAME:

WEBSITE:

USERNAME:

PASSWORD:

NOTES:

NAME:

WEBSITE:

USERNAME:

PASSWORD:

NOTES:

NAME: ______________________

WEBSITE: ______________________

USERNAME: ______________________

PASSWORD: ______________________

NOTES: ______________________

____

____

NAME: ______________________

WEBSITE: ______________________

USERNAME: ______________________

PASSWORD: ______________________

NOTES: ______________________

____

____

NAME:

WEBSITE:

USERNAME:

PASSWORD:

NOTES:

NAME:

WEBSITE:

USERNAME:

PASSWORD:

NOTES:

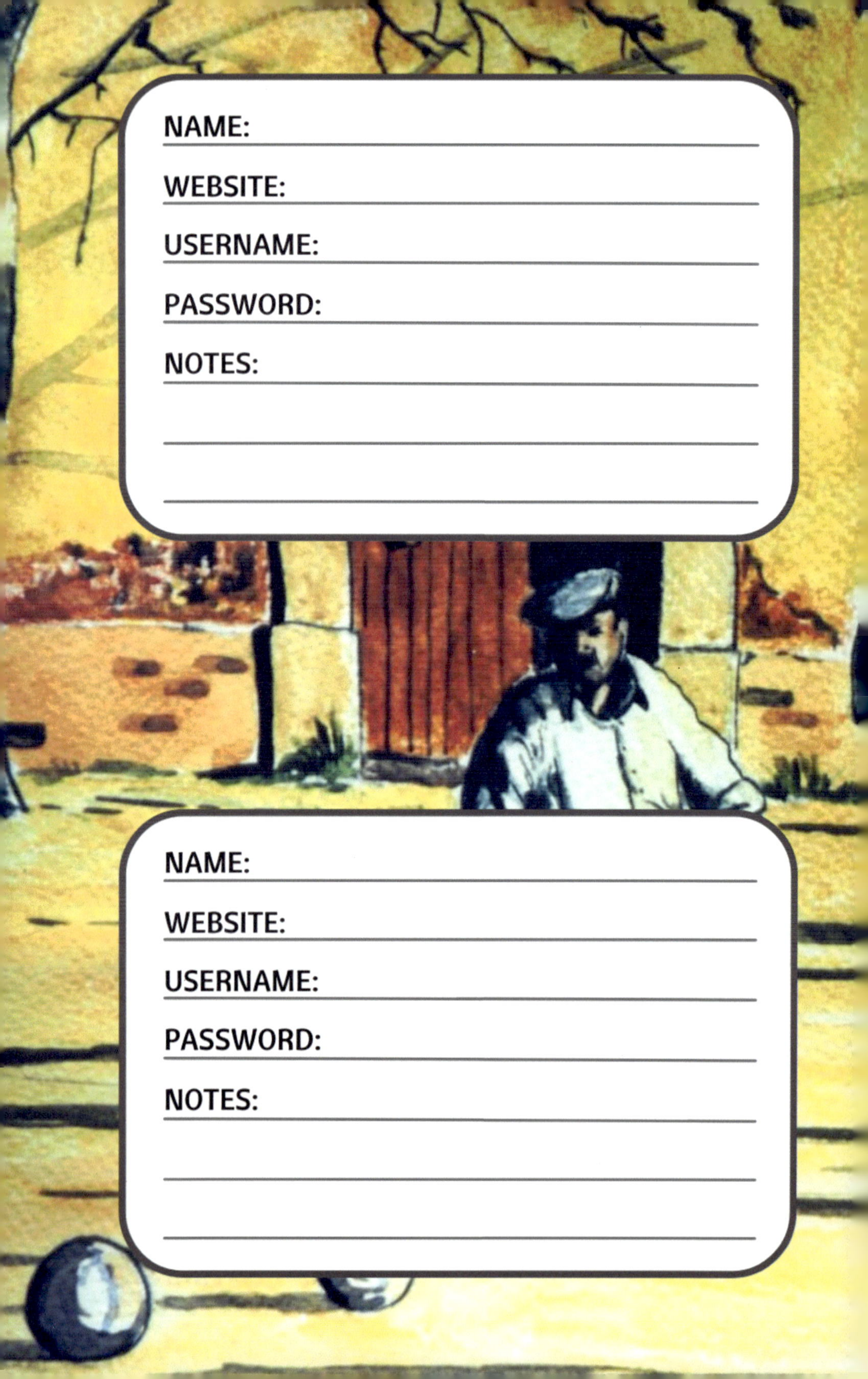

NAME:

WEBSITE:

USERNAME:

PASSWORD:

NOTES:

NAME:

WEBSITE:

USERNAME:

PASSWORD:

NOTES:

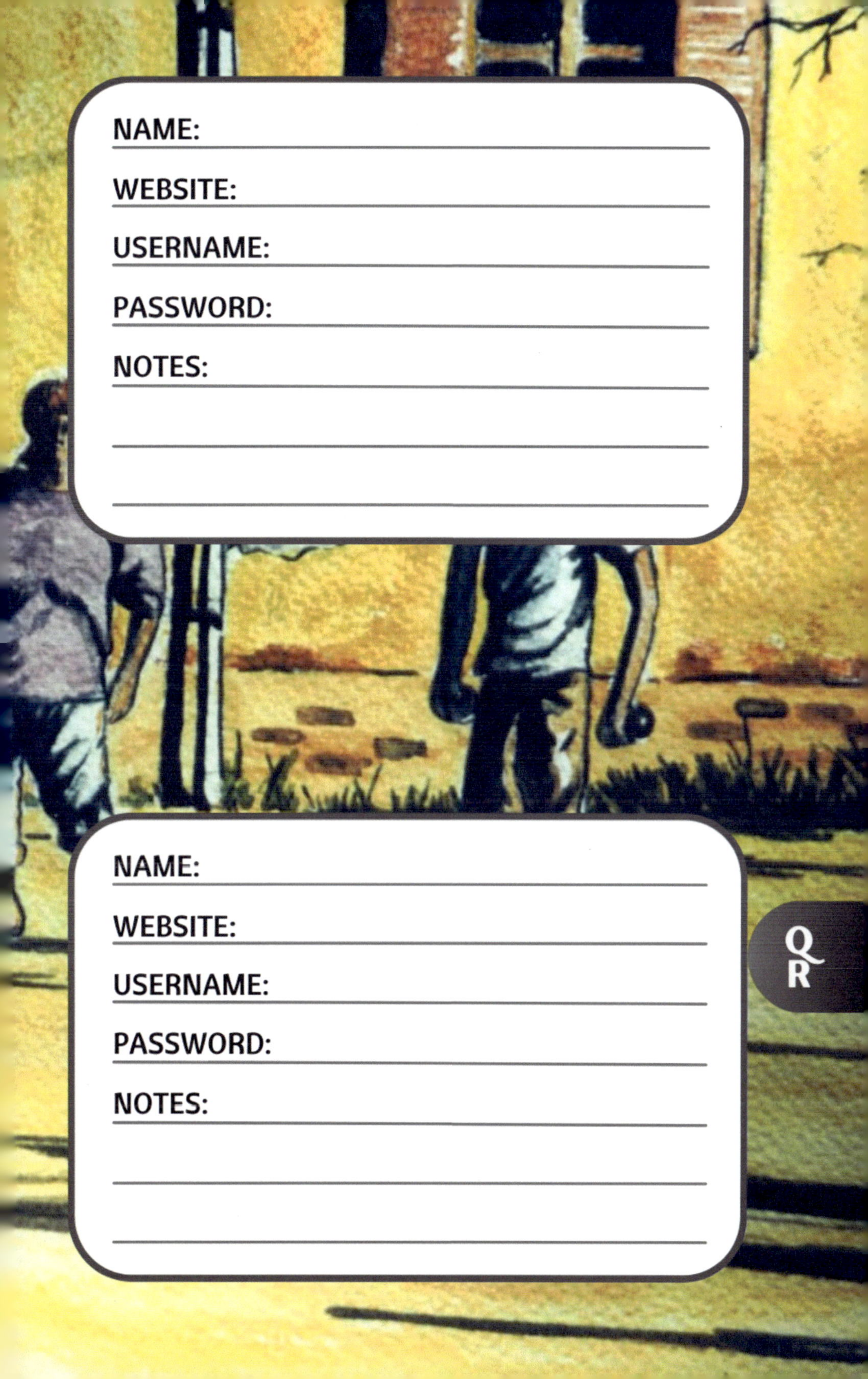

NAME: ______________________

WEBSITE: ______________________

USERNAME: ______________________

PASSWORD: ______________________

NOTES: ______________________

____

____

NAME: ______________________

WEBSITE: ______________________

USERNAME: ______________________

PASSWORD: ______________________

NOTES: ______________________

____

____

NAME:

WEBSITE:

USERNAME:

PASSWORD:

NOTES:

NAME:

WEBSITE:

USERNAME:

PASSWORD:

NOTES:

NAME:

WEBSITE:

USERNAME:

PASSWORD:

NOTES:

NAME:

WEBSITE:

USERNAME:

PASSWORD:

NOTES:

QR

NAME:

WEBSITE:

USERNAME:

PASSWORD:

NOTES:

NAME:

WEBSITE:

USERNAME:

PASSWORD:

NOTES:

NAME:

WEBSITE:

USERNAME:

PASSWORD:

NOTES:

NAME:

WEBSITE:

USERNAME:

PASSWORD:

NOTES:

NAME:

WEBSITE:

USERNAME:

PASSWORD:

NOTES:

NAME:

WEBSITE:

USERNAME:

PASSWORD:

NOTES:

NAME:

WEBSITE:

USERNAME:

PASSWORD:

NOTES:

NAME:

WEBSITE:

USERNAME:

PASSWORD:

NOTES:

NAME: ______________________

WEBSITE: ______________________

USERNAME: ______________________

PASSWORD: ______________________

NOTES: ______________________

____

____

NAME: ______________________

WEBSITE: ______________________

USERNAME: ______________________

PASSWORD: ______________________

NOTES: ______________________

____

____

NAME:

WEBSITE:

USERNAME:

PASSWORD:

NOTES:

NAME:

WEBSITE:

USERNAME:

PASSWORD:

NOTES:

NAME:

WEBSITE:

USERNAME:

PASSWORD:

NOTES:

NAME:

WEBSITE:

USERNAME:

PASSWORD:

NOTES:

NAME:

WEBSITE:

USERNAME:

PASSWORD:

NOTES:

NAME:

WEBSITE:

USERNAME:

PASSWORD:

NOTES:

S
T

NAME:

WEBSITE:

USERNAME:

PASSWORD:

NOTES:

NAME:

WEBSITE:

USERNAME:

PASSWORD:

NOTES:

NAME:

WEBSITE:

USERNAME:

PASSWORD:

NOTES:

NAME:

WEBSITE:

USERNAME:

PASSWORD:

NOTES:

NAME:

WEBSITE:

USERNAME:

PASSWORD:

NOTES:

NAME:

WEBSITE:

USERNAME:

PASSWORD:

NOTES:

NAME:

WEBSITE:

USERNAME:

PASSWORD:

NOTES:

NAME:

WEBSITE:

USERNAME:

PASSWORD:

NOTES:

NAME:

WEBSITE:

USERNAME:

PASSWORD:

NOTES:

NAME:

WEBSITE:

USERNAME:

PASSWORD:

NOTES:

NAME:

WEBSITE:

USERNAME:

PASSWORD:

NOTES:

NAME:

WEBSITE:

USERNAME:

PASSWORD:

NOTES:

NAME:

WEBSITE:

USERNAME:

PASSWORD:

NOTES:

NAME:

WEBSITE:

USERNAME:

PASSWORD:

NOTES:

NAME:

WEBSITE:

USERNAME:

PASSWORD:

NOTES:

NAME:

WEBSITE:

USERNAME:

PASSWORD:

NOTES:

UVW

NAME:

WEBSITE:

USERNAME:

PASSWORD:

NOTES:

NAME:

WEBSITE:

USERNAME:

PASSWORD:

NOTES:

NAME:

WEBSITE:

USERNAME:

PASSWORD:

NOTES:

NAME:

WEBSITE:

USERNAME:

PASSWORD:

NOTES:

NAME: ______________________

WEBSITE: ______________________

USERNAME: ______________________

PASSWORD: ______________________

NOTES: ______________________

____

____

NAME: ______________________

WEBSITE: ______________________

USERNAME: ______________________

PASSWORD: ______________________

NOTES: ______________________

____

____

NAME:

WEBSITE:

USERNAME:

PASSWORD:

NOTES:

NAME:

WEBSITE:

USERNAME:

PASSWORD:

NOTES:

NAME:

WEBSITE:

USERNAME:

PASSWORD:

NOTES:

NAME:

WEBSITE:

USERNAME:

PASSWORD:

NOTES:

NAME:

WEBSITE:

USERNAME:

PASSWORD:

NOTES:

NAME:

WEBSITE:

USERNAME:

PASSWORD:

NOTES:

NAME:

WEBSITE:

USERNAME:

PASSWORD:

NOTES:

NAME:

WEBSITE:

USERNAME:

PASSWORD:

NOTES:

NAME:

WEBSITE:

USERNAME:

PASSWORD:

NOTES:

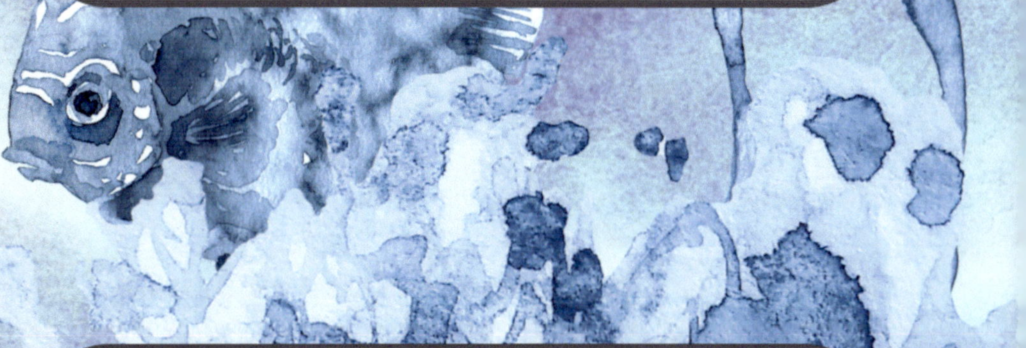

NAME:

WEBSITE:

USERNAME:

PASSWORD:

NOTES:

NAME:

WEBSITE:

USERNAME:

PASSWORD:

NOTES:

NAME:

WEBSITE:

USERNAME:

PASSWORD:

NOTES:

NAME:

WEBSITE:

USERNAME:

PASSWORD:

NOTES:

NAME:

WEBSITE:

USERNAME:

PASSWORD:

NOTES:

Made in United States
Cleveland, OH
05 November 2026

47649173R00069